THE SOUNDS OF
HEAVEN

written by:

DEBORAH TROGDON BAREFOOT

illustrated by:

ABBIE GOAN

WestBow Press books may be ordered through booksellers or by contacting:

WestBow Press
A Division of Thomas Nelson & Zondervan
1663 Liberty Drive
Bloomington, IN 47403
www.westbowpress.com
844-714-3454

Because of the dynamic nature of the Internet, any web addresses or links contained in this book may have changed since publication and may no longer be valid. The views expressed in this work are solely those of the author and do not necessarily reflect the views of the publisher, and the publisher hereby disclaims any responsibility for them.

Any people depicted in stock imagery provided by Getty Images are models, and such images are being used for illustrative purposes only.
Certain stock imagery © Getty Images.

Interior Image Credit: Abbie Goan

ISBN: 978-1-6642-7296-5 (sc)
ISBN: 978-1-6642-7297-2 (e)

Library of Congress Control Number: 2022913183

Print information available on the last page.

WestBow Press rev. date: 07/27/2022

WESTBOW
PRESS®
A DIVISION OF THOMAS NELSON
& ZONDERVAN

DEDICATION

This book is dedicated to *My Nevertheless*

(Luke 22:42 KJV)

DEBORAH TROGDON BAREFOOT

Deborah Barefoot is a retired elementary school teacher. She enjoys writing, traveling and long walks on Holden Beach.

Note From The Author

It is my hope that this book will inspire the readers to listen to the Heaven Music God sends every day.

ABBIE GOAN

Abbie Goan is a dog mom, plant lover, and an avid reader. Being an illustrator is her cherished hobby that allows her to bring entire worlds to life through her imagery.

"What does Heaven sound like?"
the little child asked one day.
"Why, Heaven sounds like music,"
her mother said.

"What kind of music?"
"All kinds."

"There's the sound of mourning doves cooing us awake from a nearby tree or the sound of thunder just before a rain shower plays its music on our rooftop."

"The buzzing of bumblebees,
a baby's sleepy cry, and the crunching
of fall leaves under our feet are
also music from Heaven."

"At Christmastime, when a choir of children sing, 'Away in a Manger,' that is Heaven music for sure!"

After thinking about all that
her mother had said,
the child asked a question.
"Do we all have Heaven music in us, then?"
"Most certainly."

"God has placed in each of us our own Heaven music. It is a gift to the world only available for us to give. We must never lose it, no matter what it may sound like to others."

"When we least expect it,
ours may be the Heaven music God
uses for someone who needs to
hear that everything will be all right."

"I see,"
the child said as she snuggled under
her covers to say her prayers.
"Tomorrow I shall listen even more."

And with that, she fell fast asleep. The peaceful rhythm of her breathing brought tears to her mother's eyes.

"Even now, my little one,"
her mother whispered,
"the sound of your breathing
is Heaven music to me."

Printed in the United States
by Baker & Taylor Publisher Services